In the Blood

Christopher Hivner

Dedication

For Mom

Miss you

Contents

This Morning

Fire burns in my fingertips
as I hold the pen,
waiting to write the words
that will save me.

In the Blood

Resting heart beats
speak to me,
languid notes
of a rhythmic song.
But it's the measures
in between
that keep me awake,
chasing away sleep
with a stricture
of my breath.
I am still,
afraid if I move
the spell of
my pulse
will be broken,
my neurons
will resist firing
leaving me a husk.
I mumble a
half-remembered psalm,
staring at the grooves
in the ceiling
for an epiphany,
truth
or a fare-thee-well.
Heart beats
speak to me,
lying,
telling me I am alive

but the measures
in between
know the truth.

Otherness

I'm flying
but not in the air,
I'm swimming
without water.
I am what happens
in the fullness of time,
the drastic measures
we take
to remain among
the living.

I am running
without legs,
I am speaking
with no tongue,
I'm joining you
in trying to become,
lusting for otherness.

Our forms remain constant
in the straight-line morning
through the deepening night.
We provide each other
what comfort we can
while we circle the sun.

I am singing to no one,
playing a march
with my bones,
looking for an audience.

Garden Stones

In the rock pile
there are remnants
of decorative stones
broken after
being tossed
with no care
on the mound.

> We talked in short bursts
> but couldn't agree.
> What I wanted
> didn't fit her skin,
> what she wanted
> sent me back home
> to the rooms on Broad Street.

I rummage
through pavement stones,
slate rocks
and earthly detritus
to find
an intact
decoration stone.

> I won't help
> dig our grave,
> she'll have to do it
> by herself.
> I step aside

to make a point
but every day
feel pushed farther
into the weeds.

I find
a molded piece
that's only broken
at one place
on one side.
I can hide
the fracture
behind a plant.

On my own,
new place,
new façade,
the flush of my skin
makes my appearance sublime.
The world watches
as I hide
my fault lines
behind written words.

Yeah, Yeah, Yeah

I'm ok
I tell myself
each morning,
the reflection in the mirror
a mask of doubt,
skepticism riding high
in my arched brow.

I'm ok
I reassure myself
with a virtual
slap on the back
and an atta-boy smile.

I'm . . . not bad
I mumble,
confidence slipping
like the hairs from my
nearly bald head.

It could be worse,
I think,
as I brush my teeth,
a collection of
bone and enamel
infiltrated by fillings
and the remnants
of a lost crown
all surrounding a lonely,

empty spot
where my favorite tooth
used to be.

It is what it is,
the catch-all
of philosophical musings,
easier to understand
than Nietzsche,
happier than Kierkegaard
even in its measured apathy.
I shrug my shoulders
and turn away
from my reflection.

I'm ok,
for now.

Carry the Day

I called to you
in a dream
while you walked through walls.
The sun lay
in the palm of your hand,
ravens circling your head
on watch for
what's to come.
I called to you
in a voice drowned by
the heart beating
in the corner of the room,
my words empty
on the air.
I wake minutes later
staring at the ceiling,
my own heart
thumping in my throat
while crows
pecked at my eyes.
I called to you
as you stood in the doorway
arms pinned by solar flares,
you called back to me
with the voice of the night,
naming me
as the one who tried.

Destiny Rides

Hitchhiking through the keystone state
down route 74
toward Maryland,
Destiny accepts a ride
with a twenty-something blonde
in a blue Mustang
who's running
from one problem to the next.
Destiny tries to sleep in the backseat
as she guns the engine
past a bored state trooper
who never bats an eye.
She lights a cigarette
with the dying butt
of the previous one
inhaling like a pro.
Then she shakes her head
in disgust
and starts talking.
Destiny pulls his jacket up
around his ears
not wanting to hear
about the ex
and the cheating and lying and drinking.
Sleep
is all he wants,
so tired of enduring
the sob stories.
After all,

he wrote them,
laid them out
for the world to take pictures of,
write books about,
argue over,
philosophize, pontificate,
accept.
Blondie chokes
on angry tears,
gesturing and
throwing glances
over her shoulder
at Destiny
who politely nods in understanding.
Her words become a tuneless buzz in his head
as he stares out the back window
at the passing stars.
The roads grow quieter
and houses fewer
as they drive deep into the country.
Blondie keeps a beer
between her legs
and endless cigs
growing from her fingers
while laying out her plan
now that she's free.
She's headed for Ocean City
to live with an old friend
who grows pot in coffee cans
and sells it to construction workers
at new hotel work sites.
Between gulps of Budweiser
Blondie invents

days on the beach,
and nights
trying on new skins
with the local boys
who won't lie to her
because she won't let them.
Destiny sighs.
he could tell her
how it's going to end
but she wouldn't listen anyway.
She finally runs out of steam
on route 1 in Delaware,
no tears or smokes left.
Destiny eventually gets some sleep
and time to dream:
everything is washed clean
in salt-water baths
that penetrate to the marrow.
The world gleams
in blanched-bone white,
pure as any temptation.
The sky splits down the middle
and folds back on itself
presenting the void,
muscular and shining
like a stallion
big enough to carry everyone
on its back.
But Destiny rides alone.
He wakes to a slap of cold air
invading through an open window.
The car has stopped
so he sits up

wiping sweat from his face
back through his hair.
After a few blinks,
recognition sets in
and he gets out of the car.
Destiny stretches his legs
at a 24-hour market in Rehoboth
as Blondie pumps
the last of her money
into the Mustang's gas tank.
The sun will be up soon
and she'll be cruising into
her new temporary life.
Destiny was never much of a
sand and surf man
so he throws a thank you to her
and she hugs him in return.
"Maybe we'll see each other again sometime," she says politely.
Destiny nods and smiles.
Walking away,
working the kinks out of
stiff, arguing legs,
he turns west.
There are Blondies everywhere
and a new one calls to him
from a house several miles inland.
A few yards down the road
he feels a familiar tug
and turns one last time.
He watches Blondie
bum enough change for cigarettes
from a sleepy,
vacationing-on-his-own-for-the-first-time teenager.

She flashes the smile
that keeps her in trouble
and will for awhile yet.
Destiny sighs
and continues down the road.

Opening a Vein

I'm filling out thank you cards
to the women
who have cheated on me,
showing my gratitude
for cutting me
so deftly
with that razor blade
and watching me bleed out.
Sliding the cards
into the envelopes
the edge of one
slices my finger
forming a line of blood
below the surface
of the skin.
The irony
is not lost on me
as I scroll eHarmony
looking for the next contestant on
this is my life.

Every Daybreak

There are remnants everywhere
I look, in every
daybreak and twilight's onset,
the lyrics of songs
and poetry's rhymes,
the faces of strangers and the
questions they ask.

The spin of the Earth
shifts me off-kilter
until I stumble down
a hillside of jagged jewels
waiting for extraction
or extinction.

At the bottom
I am even,
legs under me,
leaving the detritus behind
for a path to spring
and beyond,
to leisure and
apres-noir phantasm.

Walking through a field
of left-behind wishes
the speed of life
blurs my vision
so I move in clouds,

picking and choosing
my path
by the acid in my gut
and the tunes in my head.

There are remnants everywhere,
they don't beckon or push,
they're merely reminders
of where I've been,
cautionary trailheads
bending my light
in another direction
so I try a new path.

Slow Moving Train

The train pulled away,
starting off slow
so my eyes remained on her
for too long,
my restive tongue
almost calling out.
As the cars picked up speed
sweeping past me
like a slide show
of faces under glass
I saw the shadows
grow tall
and angled,
circus men on stilts
towering over me.
Then the clack
of the tracks
were only echoes
turned to humming,
I was still standing there
staring at the machine's ghost,
trying to remember
whether her hair was
long or short,
if her eyes penetrated
or soothed.
Finally there was silence,
I was alone
on the platform,

a mild wind
blowing through my hair,
candy wrapper
skittering along the ground.
I wanted to leave
but felt planted
in the concrete
like an ancient tree.
Voices entered my brain,
one begging me to go,
another adamant I stay
and I recognized my own tongue
screaming for me
to run after the train,
follow the rails
until I smelled her perfume again.
The perfect-backdrop sky dimmed
as night approached,
life going on around me,
strange looks
from station workers
slapped me across the face,
their voices,
filled with caution,
reach my ears as if
traveling through thick cloth.
I can't look at them
or I will collapse in tears,
I can't speak to them
or they will know
how weak I am.
The train will be back
in a few days,

maybe she will
still be on it,
her eyes searching for me,
body sweating for my touch.
The train will pull in
and I will be here
to meet it
if only as a husk
turning in the twilight.

Today Turtles

Today turtles were my favorite animal,
their shells my hiding place,
a shelter from human flesh,
loud noises and
my thoughts about everything.

Yesterday I was fond of rogue elephants
and their unpredictable power
to make people afraid,
cause the ground to shake
and be oblivious to the destruction.

I have never liked oysters,
holding onto their prize
like a spoiled child
so you have to take it by force
and then consume them as bounty.

Wolves are the perfect animal,
strong, bold and fearless.
If they were people
we'd shake their hand
instead of shooting them.

In my front yard I sit,
no shell, no power,
no prize to protect.
I'd shake your hand
but I'm afraid.

Down the Mine

There was a time
when I thought about her
all day, every day,
mining my memories
with a pick and shovel,
placing the jewels
in cloth
to protect until they
reach the surface,
the sunlight re-attaching their shine.

There was a time
when I thought about him
too often,
sneaking into the chamber
with a candle
to illuminate our past
just enough
so I'd get nicked
on a sharp edge
and bleed.

There came a time
when I tried to think
about nothing,
live in a void
of soft breezes
and esoteric things.
I boarded up the mine,

no more digging
through shards of anger,
no more cuts
too deep to suture
with a thread of deep breaths.

Now the years have passed
without subtlety.
The old helmet still fits,
new batteries in the lamp,
pick and shovel in hand,
I go mining again
searching for the gold
among the rock,
gold amidst the detritus,
gold shining its light,
gold to pay the way
to affirmation.

Storms

1. Thunder

From the porch
her eyes found him,
buzzing the side of the house
with a weedeater,
dressed in shorts
and a tanktop,
every muscle on display
and she was ashamed
to find herself preening.
A hand through the hair,
press the blouse down
so her tits
became prominent,
nipples erect
like the hook
on the fishing line.
He wouldn't look over,
didn't have to,
he knew she hated him
but that she still looked.
One pass
was all it took,
one pass
while his wife was twenty feet away
with their children,
one pass
that drained the hope from her eyes,

one pass
that made all men a disappointment,
one pass
that made her wet between her legs
and taste his sweat in her mouth,
one pass
that destroyed her.

She heard the thunder
but didn't retreat,
she wasn't scared
as she had been
when the boys
pulled her pigtails,
thunder broke the sky
but she didn't flinch
in her chair
on her porch
where she was safe
even from herself.
She was only looking
so the growl in her throat
meant nothing,
the heat from her legs
and the beads
on the meat of her breasts
were products of the
summer humidity,
the moisture in the air
that drove everyone mad,
even sensible women
who hadn't been laid
in two years

and didn't need it,
especially from him,
with his parasitic
wife and kids
who never seem to go anywhere
or do anything
that doesn't involve him
and his body.

She looked away,
into the sky.
The thunder
announced itself
with authority.

2. Lightning

The yard was immaculate
but he couldn't stop,
not yet,
she was still watching
following his every pointed move,
every flex of the bicep,
every stretch of the calf.
He felt like a bodybuilder
posing for the judges,
testosterone bubbling in his veins,
turning his mouth up
into a stupid grin
like a teenage boy
who just came for the first time
with someone else's help.

The sky lit up,
split by 500 megajoules of electricity,
he flinched,
then flexed again,
the alpha male
can't show fear
and the challenging female
was still interested.
He'd tried with her before,
but her back shot up,
something about the wife and kids,
whatever,
she kept an eye on him
and he on her,
it wasn't over yet,
he just needed to be
alone with her.
But the wife was helpless,
he had to do everything,
be everywhere,
at all times,
with her,
hold her hand,
lift her shoulders,
stroke her hair,
put her on her knees,
everything was on him,
the jagged pill
of being a man
such as he was.

He surveyed his kingdom,
hands on hips,

arm muscles dancing,
chin in the air.
Another bolt
illuminated everything.

3. Wind

The air smelled like pennies
as the rain moved in,
the tree in the front yard
fluttered its leaves
in anticipation.
The wife
had the kids occupied
so the storm
wouldn't scare them
so now she searched
for her husband,
but she didn't have to be
a bloodhound
to catch his musk
being spread
around the neighborhood,
too many
receptive bitches,
the wife was surrounded
by the heat
and couldn't fight
them all off.
He was pretending again,
this time with the lawn,
sometimes it's the car,

taking the dog for a walk,
playing with the kids,
or that he still loves the wife,
he was a born showman
for his audience of one,
prowling her porch,
displaying herself
without shame.
What was the wife to do
when they wouldn't stop?
They pushed,
time to push back.

The first rain began to fall
as the wife's eyes darkened.

4. Rain

She had been waiting
for a mist
to introduce the storm
but instead it bounded onstage
all arrogance and attitude,
sideways pellets of icy rain
struck her in the face
and a gust of wind
blew her over.
She grabbed the plastic table
as it walked across the porch,
turning it upside down,
standing on it,
looking for weight to hold it,

instead finding the wife
staring at her from the driveway,
pointing a shriveled finger,
yelling useless threats
that were lost
in the black hole of rain.
He ran over, grabbed the wife
who shoved him away,
the tiny finger
wagging at him now,
with him shouting,
more words gone,
no meaning discerned.
The wife slapped him,
he hit her back,
only much harder,
she tried for a rebuttal
but her time was up.
He was in control again,
pushing, bellowing,
hitting, demanding,
all the while looking back
and smiling at her.
She stepped off her table
and it blew away,
down the street.

Lightning played the sky
like the 4th of July,
the thunder insisting
it was the real show,
while the wind took its bows
and the rain

grew bitter and hard.
He and the wife
were still in the street,
shoving and screaming,
blaming and denying,
pleading and laughing,
while she slipped inside,
choosing not to face the storm.

Ghostly Smoke

There are memories
that leave me winded,
my breath
lost in the night air
while your face
skims the edges
of my vision.
Smells come alive
to skitter over my skin
with pin-prick feet
while I feel your hair
brush my neck,
cool tendrils
that snake
down my back.
The words you speak
form in the ether
then leave your lips
in ghostly smoke,
the sound
hollow in my ears,
drifting by
vaporous and diminishing.
This memory steals my vigor,
leaves me vacant, staring,
searching the past
for when I was strong.

Tuesday, 6:09 p.m.

At this moment,
I think
I can make it.
Right now
no words
can cleave me
nor memories
boil my bones.
I am,
in this passing second,
strong,
confident,
in command of my soul.
Now I wait
to see
what happens
when the clock
ticks over.

Monkeys with Typewriters

My attempts to write
a love song to you
have ended in a
pile-up of distended words
with no life.
These derailed trains
of superannuated metaphors
lie at the bottom
of a canyon
burning out of control.

There will be no poem
detailing my affection for you
as I am incapable
of writing one
that doesn't give me a headache.
The words I choose
mock me
with rolling eyes
and unintentional laughter,
turning my real emotion
into sardonic flotsam.

My profession of love
was to sound like Pablo Neruda,
but came out as a
Harlequin romance
generated by
monkeys with typewriters.

So the next time
we are together
I will give you a
wink and a nod,
a soft nudge in the side,
a raised eyebrow.
I will salute you
like the idiot I am
and you will know
you are loved.

Hi Fi

A song plays in my head
on a cheap, old
record player,
each pop and hiss
a ghost on my skin.
The opening of *Rats in the Cellar*
makes me twelve again
reading the liner notes
on the album jacket
while trying to understand the lyrics,
each word as big a mystery to me as
the girl in third period
I can't stop staring at.
My driving route
becomes grooves on a record,
I'm looping in circles
ever tighter,
skipping over warps
in the record,
moving closer to home.
The last song of the album
plays in my head
crackling from the tinny speakers
like a bonfire
warming my face
more than the girl
that sparkled in my eyes.
The song ends,
the needle lifts,

side one is over.
I sit in silence,
settle my eyes on row 4, seat 1
waiting for class to start.

Entropy

I took it upon myself,
all the blame,
because I couldn't find anyone else
with their hand up
waiting to be called on.

I'll make it easy for you
and admit the truth,
submit my confession,
remit my payment,
transmit a plea for clemency.

Trying for deference
I make it to martyrdom
for a cause
I'm not sure
is real.

I took it upon myself
when winter stole the sun
day after day,
cement mixer skies
and screw drivers under my nails
all to keep my earth spinning.

The Perpetual Motion Machine

Lying rigid,
the good little soldier,
she waited for him to finish and roll off.
He starts to smack her ass
as he plows through her
like a train late for the station.
She looks into his
cold, dead eyes,
black diamond mirrors.
She looked old,
too old to still have
her legs in the air for him.
But who is she then,
if not his wife?
Not a mother,
no children.
She never liked being
a sister or daughter,
not in her family.
He grunted.
The smacks were harder,
her skin felt hot.
Was it still her skin
or was it his now?
She tried to protest
but he didn't hear or didn't care.
His hands moved over her breasts
pinching and pawing.
She was getting tired,

why did it always have to hurt?
He finally came,
unloading sloppily inside of her
and over her thigh.
His eyes shined,
skaking hands with his smile,
a reptilian circle.
She lay still,
waiting for him to get off
but he just stared at her,
as though he knew
what she had been thinking.

Pixie Sticks

Lying in a ditch I found
perspective,
not of life in a bubble
but how pain directs us
down a path
we didn't know existed,
that fucks with our psyche,
tells us lies
that are sweet as pixie sticks.
I saw shapes
that taunted me,
heard voices that called me by name,
then barked at me
like my first dog.
There were snakes,
I think,
and not the metaphorical kind,
the kind that bite,
replacing your blood
with venom
and your breath
with screams.
They were there,
I think,
snakes of abnormal length and girth,
or maybe
it was a delusion,
one of the candy sticks
that left peppermint on my teeth

and a vague sense of
satisfaction + dissatisfaction.
In my ditch
I sang songs,
rock n' roll dirges
for times lost
to the foamy past,
laments for the forgotten guitar solo
and the golden-haired singer
no one could deny.
I don't think
there were snakes after all,
then again,
I don't know how
I got here,
sliding between the zebra stripes
hoping to find
the star of heaven,
but now I'm here
with snakes
or without,
sorting out the lies.

After the End

Throwing rocks
into the water,
no skipping,
just chunking,
stones disappear after a plop,
gone to the bottom to rest.
Did you ever say my name
after the end,
in a whisper or a shout,
in anger or sadness,
even joy if there was any left?
My arm is getting tired,
rocks are heavier, slippery,
covered in moss and mud,
still they sink,
a new home in the silt.
I floated for awhile
after the end,
reaching for mooring,
water in my nose,
down my throat,
birds in the trees calling to me
my only answer a wan smile.
Tossing pebbles now,
the little brothers
of the rock world,
roll between my fingers
before sending them high in the air
to watch them dive like a raptor

into the water,
gone in a barely noticeable plip.
Did you say my name
after the end,
in a rare moment,
when the lights dimmed
and supper was settled in your belly,
in a requiem or a curse,
was I there?
Throwing rocks
into the water,
praising one to float . . .

Introvert's Lament

Too many people on the trail,
crowds steal my breath,
I become small,
distant,
over.

Grave

If I fall asleep
will you come to me
in a dream
and tell me the truth?
Will you show me
my sins
in technicolor?
I can't hear you
when I'm awake,
come to me
while I'm still
as the grave
and save me.

September of '75, when I was 10

I'm shaky,
watching my steps
on the dance floor,
too many people
spilling drinks,
the lights hurt my eyes.

New grade, new teacher,
a man, first time for that,
ending day one on science.
Who wants to do
an extra credit report?
My hand goes up
before I ever think about it.
Who doesn't want extra?

I'm unstable,
don't like this music,
the DJ is speaking gibberish.
My suit is stained
and it's not mine.
Why are the lights so bright?

I get called to the front of the class.
I do my report
on a fascinating fish,
the coelacanth,
and sit down,
mentally tallying my extra credit.

The teacher walks to the front of the room
and speaks,
"That is exactly how NOT to do a report."

I'm confused
don't know why I'm here
with all these strangers,
the music is so loud
and terrible.
The DJ is wearing a bunny suit
and I'm in my pajamas,
in the spotlight
too bright.

What did you learn in school today?
That I'm a loser
who can't write an essay
about a fish.
I'm in the 5th grade now,
time to stop being a baby,
get to work,
have to do better
when you're in the big 5,
fuck the 4th grade,
time to be a man
and really learn about a fish.

Please turn the lights off,
they hurt my eyes.

Flood Tide

I'll give you a chance
if you save me,
I feel the water
rushing over,
trapped in the rocks
my body is twisted.
The waves want it all,
teeth in the white,
venom in the blue,
I am drowning in the roll.

I'll give you the benefit of the doubt
if you pull me free,
suck the water
from my throat
so I can breathe,
vanquish my sins
so God will see me.
Here comes the big wave,
a tsunami
for me, you
and the man on the island.
I'm on the reef
going down.

I'll say you were right
if you build me a boat,
a dinghy, a dhow,
trawler or yacht.

Help me ride out the storm
on a wooden slat
before the sea consumes me
and I'll make you royalty,
heir to my kingdom
of less.

I'll give you anything
if you save me from drowning
in the ocean
I created.

Rock n' Roll

Her skin blushed red
at the touch of his lips
and the taste of sweet tea
braised her tongue.
She felt herself falling
but never landed,
like a gull on the ocean
she bobbed to and fro
while he maneuvered her body.
The ceiling tiles
melted over her
like a coat of whitewash.
She spoke to a star
she knew was out there,
making a wish
that this was love,
but she knew
it was the heroin
he had juiced into her veins.
Languid and inviolate
she allowed him access
to every piece of her.
Her head filled with music
like they used to play
on the rides at the fair
when she was a child,
scratchy guitars and low voices
coming through tinny speakers.
Everything became a color with a name

and she wondered
if he put something into her wine
because she had never felt like this,
but why would he do that?
She already belonged to him,
gave everything without taking change.
If he swallowed she tried to steal it
from his throat to make it her own,
when he left her for days
she slept with his shirts
tangled between her legs,
rubbing her breasts,
covering her mouth,
suffocating.
The music became garbled in her head,
she was eating a popsicle too fast
when her mother called
and she couldn't answer fast enough,
then she was gone.
Why did he drug the wine,
is he even here?
She looked down,
her legs were still spread
and one of her nipples
was bleeding,
she reached for his hair,
felt for warmth,
the air smelled of sweet leaf
and giggled at her hands
dancing over her body
searching for her lover.
She mouthed something

to her mother
but the headache pierced her thoughts,
the popsicle had been grape,
her favorite,
she called his name.
There was no answer,
then a carnival barker
asked her to play a game,
break the balloon
win a prize,
just that easy,
and when she looked
for a dollar
she found his jacket,
sweat-stained,
soaked in cigarette smoke,
she pulled it close,
gluing it to herself
with perspiration,
petting the heavy denim
as though he were in it,
she shut her eyes
to go to sleep
and talk to her mother,
but kept her legs spread
in case he came back.

Fading From

As I left the house
I knew you weren't watching.
The last look I saw in your eyes
was denial
of the part you played,
chin in the air,
arms crossed,
you were the gallery portrait
of a self-righteous fare-thee-well.
I drove away
full in the knowledge
you were still sitting
straight-backed, legs twisted,
foot dangling and turning,
staring at that spot
on the wall
that wasn't me
or us,
living inside the wasted years,
busking for affirmation
from the paint
with the dim light of day
fading from the window.
Lean shadows
crept across the hard wood
to leave you alone
in that square room
doing math in your head
until the holy ghosts
gave you the answer.

Digging Season

The world spun under me,
the bones of others
past and further past
moaned in song
trying to tell me a secret.
Tell me a lie or a tale,
prevaricate or equivocate,
but don't tell me your secrets.
Pile the dirt high
to cover your sins,
hide each black mark
with the verve
of a king holding court.
Don't tell me your secrets,
or I'll have
to tell you mine.

2 a.m.

The phone on the wall kept
ringing
ringing
ringing
but I wouldn't answer.
I didn't want to hear her voice
unless I was looking her
in the eye,
smelling the cigarette smoke
in her clothes,
tasting the peppermint breath
as she spoke,
no more late night calls
to pull me in deeper
and keep me away
at the same time.
I'm either in
or I'm out,
the phone was
ringing
ringing
ringing
but all I heard was
my own breathing.

Across the Veldt

The fearsome lion
I want to be
is dropped in frame
by the camera
of delayed hopes.

Down the street
there is a house
where the windows
stare at you
with the malice
of the folded night.

More messages
come in
on the hour
asking if I'm the one.
I start to roar,
then go silent.

In the city
the sidewalks flood
with gnashing teeth
tearing flesh
from each other,
trading the bloody swatches
like baseball cards.

Click,
the shutter whirs,
my image captured
by the camera
of here and now,
the toothless lion
sees his face
and disappears
across the veldt.

My Darling, Perchance

Disguises aren't for everyone.
I liked to stay invisible
in front of the day
but she wanted
the fire
so we'd walk,
down the blocks, through the nationals,
me with my shoulders forward
and her a step ahead,
hair blowing in the wind
even when their wasn't any.

Old men liked to wet their fingers
when she passed by,
receiving a full set of teeth
in return,
young losers thrust their pelvis
from across the street
yelling with their hands,
spelling out filthy entreaties
with rolled tongues.
She'd stiffen her neck and pretend
she was above their distaste
but she tucked it all away
in a pocket of her flesh
to be used later.

Disguises aren't for everyone,
not for those that are even,

but she went out in layers
to collect everyone's love
so when we got home
she could be part of us
and hold that energy in reserve
in case
that wasn't enough.

Stones

I don't always do
what I'm supposed to

that's not a brag
or a regret

facts are stone
stones can be beautiful

they can also cut
or be nothing

some days I am the wind

More than Oxygen

It lay on the spoon,
flattened by her finger,
white flecks
that she needed
more than oxygen.
Her dry tongue
flicked between her lips,
a half-dead snake
anticipating nirvana.
She flicked her lighter,
moving it under the curve
of the utensil
but it didn't look right,
the fire
not the right color
and then she saw a figure
in the flame
that glowed white
and hissed,
the face was featureless
but she heard it speak:
"Don't."
She closed the lighter,
the spoon shaking
in her other hand,
her life's blood
spilling onto the table top.
Flick,
the flame sparked once more,

this time though
the figure undulated
in dark waves,
leaping at her
and laughing:
"It's all you have."
She closed the lighter,
laying the spoon down
before she dropped it.
Trembling, she caressed
the silver casing
of the lighter,
then opened it part way.
The flame was compressed,
wiggling for freedom
to grow,
reaching for the spoon
to do its job,
but around the eager
black flame
was wrapped a straining
white arm of fire
holding it back.
She lay down on the sofa
holding the lighter close,
ignoring her spoon,
denying the white net.
She closed the top,
opened it again,
closed,
open,
dazzled by the leaping flame,
orange, yellow, red, blue,

each color whispering to her.
She held it
under her hair
singeing the dirty blond ends,
the crackle
alighting in her ears,
the acrid smell
swelling in her nose.
She moved the lighter
up and down her cheek,
the flame
swaying to and fro,
licking her skin
with heat
and pain.
She closed the lighter,
opened it again
to be attacked
by her new lover
who she needed
more than oxygen.

The Islands

Chicken, flat and flavorless,
lying on the plate
like bolus in his throat,
the china in his hands,
the one pattern
he had hated,
the pattern she bought,
his opinion in the wind again,
eaten by flies
like excrement.
He stood over the sink
staring into the backyard,
watching the avatars
swim in the pool,
plant trees together,
make love on the deck
under the stars,
waving to him
from the original days,
in isolation
and unreachable,
sealed off like
an exhibit in a museum,
mocking him
from their world in the past.
The tide came in,
the tide went out,
his shoes and socks
soaked and wrapped in seaweed.

The sand shifted under him,
but he held his place.

She kept the dining room light off
so not to see the empty chair,
kept her head down
to stay blind,
tracing her fork around the flowers
on the plate
that she loved,
the pattern her mother had found
and drank with her eyes
like single malt scotch,
the pattern that made her
feel warm
and had made him
sigh with disgust
a week before the wedding,
seven days before
the rest of their lives
and she was less important
than a dinner plate.
Her finger traced
the edge of the china,
ignoring her dinner
like a finicky child,
imagining it was his shoulder
and he was on top of her,
inside of her,
a garden blooming
between them
and neither one cared.
She looked across the water

to the kitchen
for a glimpse of him,
the waves battering the dining table,
the water cold
against her bare feet,
foam slipping between her toes
and pieces of shell
laying against her skin.

From the mountain
on his island
he searched for her,
listening for the waves
to carry her voice,
but the water brought only
brine and mist.
He leaned against the sink
waiting to be led,
slapped, pushed,
a decision to be made for him
so he would go on,
pull his feet from the sand
and take a step.
The ghosts were in the house now,
walking around him
like he wasn't there,
making dinner,
putting away groceries,
sneaking a kiss on the neck.
High tide lifted the water
over his head,
drowning out his scream
for them to stop.

She collected the shells
as if they were
his kisses,
scattering them on the table,
rubbing off the sand,
pressing them to her lips
to taste the salt.
The water rose to her waist
and she floated,
allowing the current
to take her,
leaving behind her mother's plates
and the pieces of him,
letting the ocean
make her decision.
In the distance,
she thought she saw him
and tried to cry out,
but it was too far
and the waves too high.

Savior

Are you here,
have you been there,
where are you
if you aren't here or there?

I found cracks
down deep
where the oil pools
waiting for the flames
to use it up.
You can do more
than sit and wait
for Christ to return,
you have options
and emotions
and a will.
Given a choice
between the residue
and the perfume,
why is your bottle
unopened?

Are you here?

Minefields present danger
but on the other side
hands wait to wrap in yours,
words hang in the air
like confetti

to brush your skin
as they fall,
a fete to your presence.

Are you there?

Knock, knock.
Who's there?
Time rolled in cigarette paper,
one end already burning,
lying in the dirt,
discarded from nervous fingers.

Sooner, Quicker

Sooner, quicker,
that's when I need you,
right now
I wish you were here
in front of me,
aside of me,
surrounding me,
a moments' light
where your fracture
doesn't separate us,
when the devil in white
dresses in black
so you recognize him.
I could breathe again
if you'd get here
sooner, quicker.

Fence Posts

Uneven fence posts
clacking like crooked teeth
in a wind
howling between graves,
I try to squeeze between,
go untouched
by the left and the right.
Smile in the wind,
flat teeth
brittle to the coming storm,
I try to snake around
the sideways drops
to stay clean
of the lightning and the thunder.
Stumbling down the
slick grassy hill,
feet leaving the ground
like Orville and Wilbur,
I try to fly away
to avoid
double down consequences
that will rust my soul
like an old nickel.
Uneven fence posts
keeping me out,
keeping me in.

The Temptation of What Could Be

I saw the fear in your eyes
and I wanted to stay
but I knew
the look wasn't real,
all part of the game
you'd been playing
during us.
I couldn't be fooled
this time,
not if I wanted a life
where I breathe
in and out.
I wanted to stay
even in the suffocating air
and low-light dreaminess
but I saw
no mercy in your eyes
from the game you denied mastering.
Your fear
was a deception
that lured me in
over and over
despite the looseness of my blood
and the itch
in the folds of my brain,
it was a siren
for my desires,
the template of what could be.
Instead, I chose

to walk away
without a word from you,
no ploys,
no raised eyebrows
or heated skin.
As the door pulled closed
I caught only a glimpse
of your last
false look
at my ghost.

Imaginary Lines

The horizon marks me
as one
who needs help,
my boat sailing
for no shore,
no landing in sight,
paint a canvas
in the pointillist style
and I am
in every dot,
crying for the Sun to set
on the water,
melted gold
weaving a path
for me to follow
until it disappears
in the rushing darkness.
Once more
I am adrift,
the line of demarcation
out of reach
like a true
earthly purpose.
I have been marked
as someone
the continents
have no use for
and the seas
bury like treasure.

Take a fast sloop,
a rusted dhow,
fly a seaplane
from island to island,
please come for me
before the horizon
cuts me in two.

Revolutions

I rode the train all night
from the docks
to the avenues,
uptown to midtown,
past the projects
through industrial park,

and she slept next to me
for hours,
her head on my shoulder,
half-sentences
squeaking from
thin, naked lips,
her hands occasionally
grabbing at the air,
strands of soft hair
playing over
her forehead.

She had gotten on
at the avenues,
the seat next to me
the only empty,
she made a call
then was out,
sliding into my side
when we curled
past midtown,
entwining her arm

through mine,
her hand
resting on my wrist.

Between the rhythmic clacks
of the train
I inhaled
her perfume
wishing I was
whoever was in
her dream,
the man worthy
of being arm-in-arm
and receiving
her coos and moans,
not the one
who'd already pocketed
the phone
and rifled
her wallet.

I stood
to finally get off
at my stop
and she called me
Ray or Roy,
asked me
to come back to bed.

I stared at her,

wondered what
she was running from,

how many revolutions
would she make
before ending up
back home.

Scanning her phone,
I found Roy
at number two,
after mom,
left a message for him
to come and get
his girl
before she hurts herself
or someone else
does it for her.

I dropped the phone
back into her purse,
got off the train
and went home.

I fell asleep
staring at the ceiling
dreaming of gravity
and my face in the Sun.

Darlin'

He called her Sugar
then winked
with a smile that slithered.
She coughed,
choking as he tightened his grip.
He touched her hand,
called her Darlin',
ordered a second cup of coffee.
She flirted
with her bigger tip smile
never feeling his fangs
pierce her skin.
She re-filled his cup,
he told a story
about a girl he used to love
looked just like her.
He stroked her arm,
when she pulled away
he bit deeper.
She had been his wife,
high school sweethearts,
died in childbirth,
every word a lie,
but she softened.
His eyes were blue
like her dad's
and he was broken.
He called her Darlin',
this time

like it meant something.
He waited
until her shift ended,
they left together
hand in hand
his venom
coursing through her veins.

Echo

Soft rain falls
in the silence
of a deep summer night.
I feel you
thinking about me
but you're a moving target
and soon all I have
is the rain.

Bones

Cut to the chase,
motor mouth running,
gone to the north
where the problems
freeze in the cold,
let me alone
or wreck my bones,
make the decision I can't
riding with Miss Misery
and the Bad Luck Trio,
pound the drums,
no bass, no guitar,
shut the singer's mouth,
beat the drums,
bam bam bam
they can feel that in hell
and even up north
in the frozen ground.

S.O.S

God is trying to tell me something,
I can feel it
in the blood
pumping through
my wobbly heart.
A message is being sent
over waves
I can't connect to.
"Hello?"
I shout into
the empty room
waiting for a booming voice
to crack my skull.

I listen.
I listen.
I look around the room.
I look around the universe
between the points of light
in the velveteen sky.
I look into the mirror.
I close my eyes
to the surrounding everything,
exist only in the quiet moment,
I scream into the gloom.

God is trying to tell me something,
I can feel it
in the twitch

of my angry nerves.
A message is being sent,
something alive and bustling.
It's here,
under my skin,
asking for a response,
just like it has
a thousand times before.

Holy Ocean Sonata

The holy ocean
took my pulse,
returned to me
more mystery
than the day before,
left me clinging
to my beliefs
as if they were a levee
I had to rebuild.
The water
was blue with
charcoal smudges
and whitecaps
winking to my self-reliance,
the whole body
of churning water
seemed to know me,
reaching with tentacles,
open mouth waves
inviting me to join
the communion
with the holy ocean.

On the shore
I took my pulse,
the sand beneath me
shifting in ever-tightening circles,
heat from the sun
stinging my pink skin,

a reminder
of past days
spent on the promenade
my fingers curled with another.
The sand sings to me,
a siren leading me
to stay
until the tide is high,
until those fingers return
or the leviathan
swallows me whole.

The holy ocean
asks for pieces and parts
for its collection
but I am already scattered
in the sand,
buried like a
forgotten beach toy,
left behind
by voices
on the highway.

I Wrote on the Day the World Shook

The full swing
won't lay me over
until the one and only,
the firm handshake
to my look of awe,
answers the jump.

Don't say "yes, yes, yes"
or "no, no, no"
unless you've had a drink
on the rocks
and can handle
the hatred in my eyes.

I am not in love with you,
because you broke
our pact.
I am in love with you,
because I can't
break mine.

Self-deprecation,
self-introspection,
self-diagnosis,
self-denial,
put them in a bag
I'll take them with me.

My hands are like stone,
voice a raspy plea,
I am an island
surrounded by myself
a life boat floats away
just out of reach.

The Long Nights

The long-night stare
held my face,
I had no thoughts
for a pregnant moment
because it's easier
to face the truth
clear of the landfill.

The trees shimmered,
immersed in my religion
of long dead memories,
my refuge
the place that doesn't exist anymore,
even in a rock n' roll dirge.

The resurrection project
is looking for a foreman
to oversee construction
of the-past-is-never-forgotten exhibit
and I'm their man,
I can still bark out orders
mired in the sludge
of the why swamp.

Here I am
sitting on the porch
writing down my weakness
in barely legible script,
who needs a lobotomy

when all that's in front of me
is in the past.

In Your Hands

I'll give you a string of stars
for the letters in your name
if you spell out your intentions
under a fever-dream sky.
Here comes my proposal
written in the river of the Milky Way,
give your answer
with an awkward look
and breathy words,
make me wait for just . . .
one moment;
to blush my skin
and quicken my blood
because I want to be more alive
than the Sun
when you feed yourself to me.
I'll give you the light of a universe
for the darkness of your past
if you'll spell out my name
with the stars
in your hands.

A Dark Place

Find a dark place
for you and the silence
to meld
until only one of you
exists.

You are the darkness
and it is you,
but inside the belly
you'll find more
than the sum of your fear.

Inside your dark place
shallow breaths
become sustenance,
the thought of light
is an answered prayer,
time is no longer.

You are a tabula rasa
for the spirit
to imprint on,
you are a question
waiting to be asked,
a tenebrous hollow
for the light to discover.

Find your dark place,
literal and figurative,

greet the silence
with a soft tongue
and wait
for direction.

Wait for a voice
that doesn't sound
like your own,
the light may find you
in a whisper
or a roar.

Around the Edges

The sun is so bright
I see only bursts
of light,
shards of your presence
hover around the edges,
your voice
a distance
I can't measure.

The trees are green again,
spring in my pocket
like a quarter
when I need change,
if I can reach that cloud
I can gather the rain
in my hands
and you can drink.

I created the beginning,
you stole the end,
the middle
killed us both.

You remain
hovering around my edges,
a stillness in my chest,
a light that glows and dims,
your voice
stabbed by someone else's

spears of sunlight,
your presence,
unaware of its power
lingers
too long
because I ask it to.

Destination

I keep walking
but I don't know why,
my feet hurt
in the depth of the bones
and yet I can't stop.
I don't want to be here
in the ether between
where I was
and where I'm going.
I need a destination,
a map point,
a line of demarcation
for my wintery soul
to find comfort.

I keep walking,
without aid of direction
or nourishment,
into a timeline
that lacks crisp distinction.
More clouds loom on the horizon,
more agitation
for my jumpy electrons.
I am in the dark
and it is in me,
weary travelers
to a version of confusion.

When I reach the end;
a destination, a collapse,
a hole in time,
whichever greets me,
I'll bask in my journey's end.
Whether I'm standing
or kneeling
The light will shine on me
one way or the other.
When I stop walking
the light will shine.

Acknowledgements

"In the Blood" was originally published in *Underground Voices* in 2011

"Otherness" was originally published in *Anti-Heroin Chic* in 2017

"Yeah, Yeah, Yeah" was originally published in *Erothanatos* in 2019

"Carry the Day" was originally published in *Erothanatos* in 2019

"Opening a Vein" was originally published in *Record Magazine* in 2018

"Every Daybreak" was originally published in *Erothanatos* in 2019

"Slow Moving Train" was originally published in *Dead Snakes* in 2015

"Today Turtles" was originally published in *Eye on Life* in 2014

"Down the Mine" was originally published in *Song of Eretz* in 2015

"The Islands" was originally published in *Song of Eretz* in 2015

"Monkeys with Typewriters" published in *Song of Eretz* in 2015

"Hi Fi" was originally published in *Pyrokinetic* in 2016

"Entropy" was originally published in *Black Mirror Magazine* in 2013

"The Perpetual Motion Machine" was originally published in *Yellow Mama* in 2011

"Grave" was originally published in *Record* in 2019

"Rock n' Roll" was originally published in *Underground Voices* in 2010

"Digging Season" was originally published in *Yellow Mama* in 2017

"2 a.m." was originally published in *Record Magazine* in 2019

"My Darling, Perchance" was originally published in *Anti-Heroin Chic* in 2016

"Stones" was originally published in *Eye on Life* in 2012

"More than Oxygen" was originally published in *Yellow Mama* in 2012

"Sooner, Quicker" was originally published in *Culture Cult Magazine* in 2018

"Imaginary Lines" was originally published in *Ephemera* in 2017

"Revolutions" was originally published in *Dead Snakes* in 2011

"Darlin" was originally published in *Underground Voices* in 2011

"Bones" was originally published in *Yellow Mama* in 2019

"S.O.S." was originally published in *Record Magazine* in 2018

"Holy Ocean Sonata" was originally published in *Of Sun and Sand Anthology* in 2013

"I Wrote on the Day the World Shook" was originally published in *CC&D* in 2017

"Around the Edges" was originally published in *Bigger Stones* in 2013